# *Advance Praise*

"Karsonya Wise Whitehead has that rare ability, the God-given gift, to electrify a room with moral purpose, intellectual clarity, and historical insight. She occupies the summit of the Black intellectual as moral leader and galvanizing force. Those of us who attended the 2013 Carter G. Woodson Lecture in Jacksonville, Florida, fell under her spell as she wove the history of the black struggle for freedom and equality from the Emancipation Proclamation to the March on Washington. "Sparking the Genius" is a gem that illuminates the African American struggle in the United States."
— Daryl Michael Scott, Professor of History
Howard University, and President of ASALH

"2014 marks the 50th anniversary of the Civil Rights Act. In "Sparking the Genius," Dr. Karsonya Whitehead expands upon the speech she gave at the 2013 Carter G. Woodson Lecture (ASALH conference in Jacksonville, FL). She takes us back to the early Civil Rights Movement (the release of the Emancipation Proclamation) and then moves us to the modern Civil Rights Movement. In the dynamic oratory voice of her father, who is a pastor, Whitehead challenges us to (re)spark the genius in not only ourselves, but to also spark this genius in those we come in contact with, especially the youth.

"Sparking the Genius" is not just a challenge, but also a call for action in all of us to see beyond today and work toward the future. This is indeed wise counsel from a brilliant young scholar."

– Janet Sims-Wood, Ph.D.
National VP for Membership of ASALH

"Sparking the Genius is a riveting call to action from Dr. Whitehead to all generations to fully embrace and learn from our Black History and Heritage. If we are to obliterate oppressive thinking we must be aware of the repetitive racial injustices and social movements to eradicate them. We must be vigilant in our quest to learn from and educate others about our past and vehemently take charge to direct our future course."

– Cheryl Clark, CEO
National Visionary Leadership Project

CARTER G. WOODSON LECTURE 2013

Sparking the Genius
Karsonya Wise Whitehead

CARTER G. WOODSON LECTURE 2013

Sparking the Genius
Karsonya Wise Whitehead

Apprentice House
Loyola University Maryland
Baltimore, Maryland

First Edition

Printed in the United States of America

ISBN: 978-1-62720-012-7
Ebook ISBN: 978-1-62720-013-4

Book Design by Kevin Atticks
Cover Illustration by Calvin Coleman
Edited by Ronald D. Harrison, Jr.

Published by Apprentice House

Apprentice House
Loyola University Maryland
4501 N. Charles Street
Baltimore, MD 21210
410.617.5265 • 410.617.2198 (fax)
www.ApprenticeHouse.com
info@ApprenticeHouse.com

# *meditations*

*(dedicated to my children—Mercedes, Kofi, & Amir—to spark their genius)*

Commit yourself to being…

Hope for those who have none
A lighthouse in the midst of a storm
A compass that points the way

A road that diverges from the well-worn path
A safe-house for those who need a resting place
An inn that is never full

A scholar in pursuit of new questions
A pilgrim in search of the *magis*
A voice that speaks the truth

A light that finds its way into every corner
A gear that shifts and moves us forward
A life that is well-lived

Commit yourself to be-ing
Commit yourself to be
Commit yourself

And then, in the end, just
Commit

# *Acknowledgements*

I was five years old when I gave my first speech. The church hosted a yearly children's programs and I was scheduled to recite two Bible verses. My father practiced every night to help me to remember. On Saturday nights, he would have me stand in the living room and pretend that I was speaking at the White House or before the United Nations or on national television. He would introduce me and have me come forward, give a little curtsy, say my name, and then recite my verse. He told me that I needed to get into the habit of always being ready to speak out and speak up. He used to call it the art of "intensely waiting but casually listening," so that no matter where I was or who was speaking, I was always prepared to speak. He told me that I had a gift for the spoken word and that even when I was born, while most babies cried, I moved my mouth trying to say something as if I wanted to mark the moment. I stating talking then and have not stopped since.

I heard my first Carter G. Woodson Lecture three years ago when I was starting my second year as an assistant professor. I attended the annual convention for the Association for the Study of African American Life and History (ASALH), and I was amazed and humbled to be in the presence of so many scholars, teachers, and activists who loved and supported African-

American history. The conference was held in Raleigh, NC, and the speaker was Evelyn Brooks Higginbotham. I knew her name and had used her research in my dissertation. I sat there, practicing the art of intensely waiting and casually listening, and was moved by her message and her challenge to the audience. I remember that at that moment one of my dreams was to someday be selected to give that prestigious and historic lecture. Fast forward three years to when Dr. Daryl Michael Scott, ASALH's president elect, called me to invite me to do what I had only dreamed of doing, stand on the stage where historians whose words had inspired me to major in and study African-American history, had stood. The Woodson Lecture is the type of lecture that I have been preparing to give all of my life, and I am grateful to have been able to do so. There are some events that mark the life of a historian: the moment you decide to major in history, the first time you make a historical argument or write a historiography, the day you defend your dissertation, the publication of your first monograph, and the day when you are asked to give a foundational lecture in the field.

As I prepared to give the Woodson Lecture, there were a number of people who supported and encouraged me along the way. I am particularly grateful to Dr. Daryl Michael Scott and Sylvia Cyrus, ASALH's Executive Director, who selected me and encouraged me along the way; and, Dr. La Vonne Neal for her amazing introduction, her support, and her ongoing encouragement. Cheryl Clarke, Dr. Conra Gist and Dr. Regina Lewis were both patient and kind as they helped me to prepare for the Lecture. I am also thankful and grateful to La Vonne and her writing partner, Dr. Alicia Moore, and to Conra for contributing to the final project. My assistant, Megan Fisher, has been working with me for the past three years and is an

invaluable part of my writing and editing process. I am delighted
that she has contributed a written piece to the final product. I
am humbled by Calvin Coleman's talent and by his willingness
to paint the cover for the book. His only request was that he
would be able to paint Woodson the way that *he* saw him; and
now when I look at the cover, I cannot imagine seeing Woodson
any other way. My copy editor, Ronald D. Harrison, Jr., and my
publisher, Kevin Atticks, generously supported me and assisted
me in getting the speech from my head onto paper. My parents,
Carson and Bonnie Wise, have never wavered in their support of
my dreams and goals. My children—Mercedes Alexandria, Kofi
Elijah, and Amir Elisha—once again acted as my armor bearers
and cheerleaders. The understanding, patience, and love from
my husband, Johnnie, provides the wind that I need to soar and
fly. As always, any work that I do is for him.

Karsonya Wise Whitehead
*Baltimore, MD*

*December 1, 2013*

*Reflections:*
*On Writing The Carter G. Woodson Lecture*

*Sparking the Genius:*
*The 2013 Carter G. Woodson Lecture*
Karsonya Wise Whitehead

# Contents

# Alicia L. Moore & La Vonne Neal

*"Keep on Pushing: There Will Always Be a Next Time"*

Karsonya Wise Whitehead's Woodson lecture, "The Moral Arc of Justice: Shifting Narratives, Sparking Genius, and Learning How to See Beyond," opened in the spirit of Theodore Parker and Dr. Martin Luther King, Jr., who both spoke to the prophetic vision needed to see the moral arc of the universe.[1] As explained in Parker's words, "The arc is a long one. My eye reaches but little ways. I cannot calculate the curve and complete the figure by experience of sight. I can divine it by conscience. And from what I see, I am sure it bends toward justice."[2] This metaphor Whitehead used to frame the struggles and triumphs of the Civil Rights Movement— from the Emancipation Proclamation to the release of Dr. King's letter and the March on Washington—reminds us of the freedom fighters who had the vision to get us there—Woodson, King, Hughes, Baldwin, Height, and Bethune. As Whitehead's father once said,

"Freedom is something that we have to go and get," if we keep moving—towards freedom, towards something better, towards the end.

Most importantly, Whitehead's father taught her how to spark genius in African-American youth—young boys and girls—so we can turn them into scientists, doctors, lawyers, and get them from prison into college. This speaks to the power of teaching history for social justice to our current generation of students—so we can undo the fact that forty-seven percent of African-American males drop out of high school, so we can undo the mass incarceration of African-American males. The school-to-prison pipeline must be dismantled. We must remember that we are a part of this country's soil, ASALH family.

Whitehead's lecture teaches us to cherish the bittersweet memories of African-American history—born out of struggle and filled with agonizing prayers; they are teeming with hope, pushing for justice, and shifting the global consciousness. This beautiful metaphor—the moral arc of the universe—Whitehead alluded to as a tool to express the significance of the events which created "shifts in the universe," such as bus boycotts, lunch-counter sit-ins, and peaceful, non-violent protests.

The implications of Whitehead's lecture for African-American life and education are profound and rooted in the hope of what is to come. As James Baldwin wrote in his open letter to his nephew:

> ...for this is your home, my friend. Do not be driven from it. Great men [and women] have done great things here and will again and we can make America *what America must become* [emphasis is author's]. It will be hard, James, but you come from sturdy peasant stock, men [and women] who picked cotton, dammed rivers, built railroads, and in the teeth of the most terrifying odds, achieved an unassailable and monumental dignity.[3]

Despite recent setbacks with the Zimmerman travesty, the repeal of sections of the Voting Rights Act, and the gentrification of Black neighborhoods and schools, we must remember that there will always be a next time. So if we can't be at the table when freedom comes, we must make sure our children will be, and that is a promise of culturally responsive pedagogy. Thus, we must remember our responsibilities to teach African-American history in our homes and our schools; we must remind our children about the triumphs of the Civil Rights Movement. We must educate for social justice so that we can eradicate systems of subjugation. As a result, we educate to eliminate poverty; we educate to make this world a more peaceful place for our gay brothers and sisters; we educate to transform inequalities in the workplace. This is how we learn to see beyond—beyond the silenced boundaries of oppression; beyond race, class, and gender barriers; beyond the intersections of multiple subjectivities. Freedom is something we must run and get. How long will it take to see social justice? Dr. King said, "Not long, because the arc of the moral universe is long, but it bends toward justice."[4] Whitehead invoked the spirit of Dr. Martin Luther King, Jr., who reminded us that we are caught in a "network of mutuality, tied in a single garment of destiny. Whatever affects one directly, affects all indirectly."[5] Remember that if we do not educate for social justice, future generations will destroy themselves. Our moral responsibility is to spark the genius, as Dr. Carter G. Woodson, the founder of ASALH and Black History week, instructed us to do.

Imagine living in a world where college students do not get pepper-sprayed for assembling peacefully, where black men are not pulled over for driving or walking while black, where African-American teenagers can walk safely through white neighborhoods without the fear of being shot, where American citizens living in public housing do not fear being displaced and becoming homeless because of gentrification. This is a world worth educating for and fighting for, no matter how weary we become. Let us make sure our youth have a seat at the table when freedom comes. Whitehead's 2013 Carter G. Woodson Lecture inspires us to keep pushing forward; it sparks our genius, forces us to think, to dream, and to ultimately move beyond what our eyes can see.

# *Megan Fisher*

*"We should emphasize not Negro History,*
*but the Negro in history."*[6]

Carter Godwin Woodson (19 Dec. 1875 – 3 April 1950), writer, and founder of Negro History Week and the Association of African American Life and History (ASALH), was one of nine children born to James Henry Woodson and Anna Eliza Riddle in New Canton in Buckingham County, Virginia. He spent his early years with his parents, working as a farm laborer and attending school at a one-room schoolhouse where his uncles taught. At the age of seventeen, he relocated to Fayette Country to work as a coal miner. Less than three years later, he enrolled in segregated Douglass High School in Huntington, West Virginia, graduating two years later with his high school diploma. He went on to attend Berea College, an integrated school that had been founded by the Quakers in Kentucky, earning his Bachelor of Literature degree in 1903. After college, Woodson moved to the Philippines to work as an education superintendent on behalf of the U.S. government, returning five years later to attend the University of Chicago. He earned both an A.B. degree and an A.M. in European History and then enrolled in a doctoral program at Harvard University. In 1912, when he received his degree in history, he became only the second African-American to earn a doctoral degree from

Harvard. (W.E.B. Du Bois was the first, receiving his Ph.D. in 1895.) Woodson is believed to be the first person of enslaved parents to receive a Ph.D. in history from any university.

After completing his formal studies, Woodson taught at a public high school in Washington, DC, and during this time, he continued to research the history of African Americans. There are a number of theories that attempt to explain why he was so focused on African American history: maybe because he believed that it was being completely ignored by historical scholars, or maybe he believed that those who conducted research in this area were misrepresenting the history, or maybe it was because he simply had an overwhelming desire to tell the history of his people. In either case, Woodson's commitment to researching and sharing the history of African Americans, as evidenced by his publications, was unparalleled at that time. In 1915, while the country was celebrating the fiftieth anniversary of the release of Abraham Lincoln's Emancipation Proclamation, Woodson began to establish himself as a forefather of African-American life and culture. While attending the Exposition of Negro Progress in Chicago, Woodson founded the Association for the Study of Negro Life and History (which later became ASALH, the Association for the Study of African American Life and History). The following year he established the *Journal of Negro History* (currently the *Journal of African American History*), an academic journal in which African-American scholars who were barred from publishing in mainstream historical (white) journals could write and share their research on and about African-American life and history. He also co-published his first book, *The Education of the Negro Prior to 1861*, a broad historiography that traced the lives and experiences of African Americans in the United States from the beginning of slavery through the end of the Civil War.

Three years later, after gaining a name and an audience for himself as a traveling lecturer on African American history as well as hosting annual meetings of his Association, Woodson published his second book, *A Century of Negro Migration*. In it, he discussed the movement of African Americans within the United States and the effects it had on race relations. This was the beginning of a very productive period of writing and publishing for Woodson. By 1921, he was working with African-American teachers to promote the teaching of African-American history; and he formed the Associated Publishers Press, an African-American owned book-publishing house. Later that year, his book, *The History of the Negro Church*, which chronicled the emergence of African-American churches and the changes that occurred within them between the eighteenth and twentieth centuries, was published. In 1926, he published *The Mind of the Negro as Reflected in Letters Written During the Crisis, 1800-1860,* which used primary documents from church missions, anti-slavery societies, and personal papers to explore the stories and experiences of African Americans during the sixty years before the Civil War; and he organized the first Negro History Week in February, connecting it to the birthday of both Frederick Douglass and of Abraham Lincoln. Fifty years later, this one-week informal celebration was officially recognized and expanded into a month—becoming known as Black History Month—by the U.S. government.

By 1933, Woodson had become a fixture on the lecture circuit and was writing and publishing books and articles, including his seminal work, *The Mis-Education of the Negro*. In this book, which has become his most well-known publication, Woodson theorized and offered evidence that African Americans were being indoctrinated, but not taught, at American schools during this time. It has been suggested that Woodson's theories on how African-American students were being mis-educated are as true today as they were when he first published this work. In total, Woodson published approximately thirteen single-authored books that focused on African-American history. Additionally, he was actively involved in the struggle for civil rights, working with the National Association for the Advancement of Colored People (NAACP) (though he later ended his affiliation) and with Marcus Garvey's United Negro Improvement Association, becoming a writer for Garvey's *Negro World*. During this time, he also worked as a principal for the Armstrong Manual Training School in Washington, DC, and later served as a college dean at Howard University and then at West Virginia Collegiate Institute. In 1937, Woodson founded the *Negro History Bulletin* (currently the *Black History Bulletin*), a journal for middle and high school teachers, which has recently become the nation's oldest continuously published journal for practitioners.

Woodson left a legacy through his efforts as a dedicated scholar, historian, and author. He spent his life emphasizing the importance of education and researching and sharing the previously ignored history of African Americans. His achievements—including the founding of ASALH, the publication of *The Mis-Education*, and the establishment of Negro History Week—profoundly changed the course of American history by ensuring that the stories by and about African Americans would not be forgotten or misinterpreted. Although Woodson died in 1950, his life and his legacy continues to inspire, encourage, and challenge young scholars of African-American and American history.

# *Reflections:*
# *On Writing*
# *The Carter G. Woodson Lecture*

*"road maps to guide us along the way"*

The purpose of my Carter G. Woodson Lecture was to provoke thoughts, ideas, and conversations about the ways in which we think about emancipation and freedom. Although there are major differences between what I originally wrote (which is the version presented here) and what I delivered (which is available for download online), they build on one another and on the same premise. Essential to both is the notion that in 1963 there were some Critical Moments that happened within the black community that profoundly shaped the direction of the Civil Rights Movement. An example of this is the impact that the Birmingham Campaign had on President John F. Kennedy and how it shaped his decision to both intervene in the conflict and draft the 1964 Civil Rights Act. By further example one can look at the impact of the release of Dr. King's "Letter from a Birmingham Jail," which traced the history of nonviolence as a political strategy from Jesus Christ to James Farmer and which has since become a moral edict for our nation. In addition to the

Birmingham Campaign and the release of the "Letter," the Critical
Moments that I examine include the assassination of Medgar
Evers, the March on Washington for Jobs and Freedom, and the
bombing of the Sixteenth Street Baptist Church. The long term
impact of these Critical Moments, in addition to the drafting of
the 1964 Civil Rights Act, include both the passage of the 1965
Voting Rights Act and the 1968 Civil Rights Act. So with these
Critical Moments in mind, I suggest that 1963 is a year that
requires close consideration and study as one begins to research
and deconstruct the Civil Rights Movement.

At the same time, I argue that the Critical Moments that
happened in 1963 are uniquely connected to a Critical Moment
that happened 100 years earlier in January 1863. It was during
the third year of the U.S. Civil War that Abraham Lincoln, in
a desperate attempt to force Confederate states to rejoin the
Union or risk losing their enslaved population, decided to release
his Emancipation Proclamation. It was a pro-war document
and not a statement or declaration in support of ending the
peculiar American system of perpetual slavery. Even though the
Proclamation did not legally free anyone, it did lead to freedom.
I offer by way of an example an assumption that was posited by
Jacqueline Jones Royster who argued that emancipation "was
not a gift bestowed upon passive slaves by Union soldiers or
presidential proclamation; rather, it was a process by which black
people ceased to labor for their masters and sought instead to
provide directly for one another" as well as the work of Ira Berlin
who notes that by running away and freeing themselves, "the
actions of the slaves made it possible and necessary for citizens,
legislators, military officers, and the president to act."[1]

---

1. Royster, Jacqueline Jones. *Traces of a Stream: Literacy and Social Change among African American Women.* Pittsburgh: University of Pittsburgh Press, 2000, 46; Ira Berlin, *Who Freed the Slaves? Emancipation and Its Meaning, in Major Problems in the Civil War and Reconstruction,* 2nd ed., ed. Michael Perman (New York: Houghton Mifflin Company, 1998), 291.

By framing emancipation and freedom as something that black Americans had to go and get for themselves rather than viewing it as something that was given to them, expands our understanding of how the release of the Emancipation Proclamation in 1863 is connected to the Critical Moments of 1963. During both of these years, black people were fighting for, claiming, taking, and finding ways to redefine the notions of freedom. In 1863, freedom meant the end of American slavery; and, in 1963, it meant the end of "Jim Crow." In both cases, black Americans had to work for and vigorously pursue the elusive state called freedom.

The Woodson Lecture also takes seriously the "charge" that was given by Carter G. Woodson in his 1936 book, *The Mis-Education of the Negro*. In it, he argued that black students were not being properly educated in the school system:

> The same educational process which inspires
> and stimulates the oppressor with the thought
> that he is everything and has accomplished
> everything worth while, depresses and crushes
> at the same time the *spark of genius* in the
> Negro by making him feel that his race does
> not amount to much and never will measure
> up to the standards of other peoples. The Negro
> thus educated is a hopeless liability of the race.
> [Emphasis added][2]

Our goal then, as educators and as a community, is to be committed to working to "spark the genius" in the young people around us. I believe that there is a place that exists beyond our current reality, beyond our unfulfilled dreams and broken promises, beyond poverty and crime and illiteracy and abuse,

---

2. Woodson, *The Mis-Education of the Negro*, 4-5.

a place that exists —only at this moment— in our dreams. A place that we can only get to by sparking genius, shifting gears, and changing the current narrative. Both the Woodson lecture and the essay are designed to be used as road maps to guide us along the way.

Sparking the Genius

The 2013 Carter G. Woodson Lecture

# *Karsonya Wise Whitehead*

*"Spark my genius, set me on fire and set me loose into the world."*[1]

It is wonderful to be here in Jacksonville, Florida, in a room full of people who believe in and love black history and who actively support the Association for the Study of African American Life and History, our beloved ASALH. We stand here two years away from celebrating their centennial, and we are excited that ASALH not only continues to be a lighthouse, safely guiding ships into the shore, but it also continues to stand as a gateway, guarding and protecting our history. I am honored to have been asked to bring the Carter G. Woodson Lecture, knowing that those who have come before me have blazed a trail of excellence and brilliance. I stand here on their shoulders, grateful for all that they have done. They have shown us how to walk with our heads held up high, looking forward, knowing that we may not yet see the end, but we are confident that we are going to get there, and we need to get there together.

I want to talk to you today about "The Moral Arc of Justice: Shifting Narratives, Sparking Genius, and Learning How to See Beyond." In 1853, Unitarian minister and abolitionist Theodore Parker of Massachusetts said,

> I do not pretend to understand the moral
> universe. The arc is a long one. My eye reaches
> but little ways. I cannot calculate the curve and

complete the figure by experience of sight. I can
divine it by conscience. And from what I see, I
am sure it bends toward justice.[8]

In 1965, one hundred twelve years later, in a speech in
Selma, Alabama, Dr. King was asked, How long will it take to
see social justice? He answered:
I come to say to you this afternoon, however
difficult the moment, however frustrating the
hour, it will not be long, because truth crushed
to earth will rise again. How long? Not long,
because no lie can live forever. How long? Not
long, because you shall reap what you sow. How
long? Not long, because the arc of the moral
universe is long, but it bends toward justice.[9]

We are standing here at the crossroads of emancipation
and freedom during a year that we have celebrated and
commemorated black history moments from the release of the
Emancipation Proclamation on January first to the bombing
at the Birmingham Church on September fifteenth. We are at
an interesting time in American history because the arc that
Dr. King and Theodore Parker talked about is still bending. It
may not be bending as quickly as we would like, but it is still
bending. We have not yet gotten to that place where the valleys
have been exalted, the hills and mountains have been made low,
the rough places made plain, and every crooked place has been
made straight.[10] "The universe," as King once said, "is on the
side of justice," but I believe that justice is taking a long time
to get here.[11] During this same year of historical anniversaries,
we have seen the impact of the rulings in both the *Florida v
Zimmerman* and the *Shelby v Holder* cases.[12] We have also borne

witness to the fact that forty-seven percent of African-American males across the country are dropping out of high school and dropping out of society.[13]

*Justice* is taking a mighty long time to get here.

We are living in a time when black men are being shot simply because they are committing the crime of breathing and moving and being while black. The "classroom-to-prison" pipeline has yet to be disrupted and dismantled, and eighty-four percent of African-American fourth graders are still reading below grade level.[14]

*Justice* is taking a mighty long time to get here.

We have a great responsibility because as the arc is bending, those of us who know the history or have lived the history or have studied the history must be charged with the responsibility of teaching the history. We must share our knowledge to ensure that the generations to come will not continue to be destroyed simply because they have not learned their history or, worse yet, they have rejected it. We must do our part to spark their genius—the genius that Dr. Carter G. Woodson, the founder of ASALH and Negro History Week, was talking about in his book, *The Mis-Education of the Negro*—and as we do that we must also seek to spark that genius in ourselves as well.[15]

I stand here today as someone who was spoon-fed stories about black history. I used to get my peas, corn, and stories about the Civil Rights Movement at the same time. I remember saying, more than once, "Pass the biscuits, Daddy, and tell me what happened at the March." I would sit at my father's feet as a child and listen to stories about marching and singing, preaching and praying, and sacrifice and struggle. My father is a Baptist minister, and he used to challenge me as a child, saying, "I want you to memorize entire books of the Bible and speeches by

Dr. King. I want you to memorize poetry by Langston Hughes, Sonia Sanchez, and Gwendolyn Brooks. I want you to learn the words from the songs of Sweet Honey in the Rock. I challenge you to memorize those types of things." He would plaster my walls with pictures of beautiful brown people so that the last image I saw at night and the first image I saw in the morning was of people that looked like me.

He used to tell me that his job as my father was not just to purchase my shoes and clothes, but it was also to spark my genius, set me on fire, and then set me loose into the world. He said that I was supposed to be like David, who ran to meet Goliath, confident that one stone would knock down a giant. I was supposed to be able to speak to a mountain that was in my way and tell it to move, and it would be gone. My father taught me that when genius is sparked, giants start to fall and mountains begin to move. The word "genius" in ancient Rome actually meant, "to bring into being, to create, or to produce." In early 63 BC, during the time of Augustus, the word "genius" acquired a secondary meaning, which was "inspiration" or "talent." Genius, therefore, is not something that you are necessarily born with; it is a goal. It is something that you can work to achieve. It is attainable, and it is something that sits right out there in front of you.

You can spark genius in young boys and turn them into scientists.

You can spark genius in young girls and turn them into doctors.

We can spark genius in young people and get them from the prison into college.

We can change lives if we believe we can.

You and I, we must spark our genius and then spark the

genius of the young people around us. They have to believe
that justice is something that they can get. They have to believe
that they can make a difference regardless of their age, their
circumstances, or their history. They must be told that their
history does not have to determine their destiny even though
their history is a part of their destiny.

When genius is sparked and history is taught, young people
are inspired. I believe that when that happens, gears begin to
shift somewhere in the universe. Eldridge Cleaver once said that
when Rosa Parks sat down, somewhere in the universe a gear in
the machinery shifted.[16] When decisions are made, genius is
sparked, and history is taught, gears begin to shift and things
are set into motion. The gears shifted when Rosa Parks did not
get up, but they were set into motion, months earlier when
Claudette Colvin did not get up.[17] They shifted when Harriet
Tubman chose to leave, but they were set into motion when her
parents and her family chose to stay. When gears shift, things
begin to happen.

This year alone we have celebrated many of those gear-
shifting, life-changing moments. In January, we celebrated
the 150th anniversary of the Emancipation Proclamation—a
document that, at the time it was released, did not actually "free"
anyone. Abraham Lincoln did not have the means or the ability
to actually enforce it in the states that were in active rebellion
against the Union; but when we think about it today, we mark
it as a significant moment—a moment when freedom became
real and attainable whereas before it was something the enslaved
prayed about, hoped for, or figured they would die before they
got it. After January 1, 1863, freedom was something they
could run out and get and it was something that was important
to them.

On December 31, 1862, the night before the document was released, many were nervous, unsure that Lincoln was going to go forward with his plan. In Boston, Massachusetts, at the Tremont Church—the same place that Dwight L. Moody once called America's pulpit—Frederick Douglass, along with orator and women's suffragist Anna Dickinson and slave narrative author and historian William Wells Brown, held a public meeting to countdown the moments before the release. In his speech, Douglass, in an emotionally charged address, spoke about what this moment meant for all Americans:

> We were waiting and listening as for a bolt from
> the sky, which should rend the fetters of four
> million slaves; we were watching as it were, by
> the dim light of stars, for the dawn of a new
> day; we were longing for the answer to the
> agonizing prayers of centuries. Remembering
> those in bounds and bound with them, we
> wanted to join in the shout for freedom, and in
> the anthem of the redeemed.[18]

When that moment—the one that King called "a great beacon light of hope to millions of slaves who had been seared in the flames of withering justice"—came and the Emancipation Proclamation was released, it was seen as a "daybreak that ended their long night of captivity," and when this happened a gear shifted somewhere in the universe, and the world was never the same.[19] As one enslaved woman said when she heard that Lincoln "done signed" the Emancipation, "I started out with blankets and clothes and pots and pans and chickens and hens and corn and I ran out to meet the Union army" because when they were coming, it now meant that freedom was coming with them.[20] Freedom was something you ran out to get. Gears shifted, consciousness changed, shackles were removed; minds were emancipated from mental slavery.

We also marked the fiftieth anniversary of the release of Dr. King's "Letter from a Birmingham Jail." It was on April second that the Alabama Christian Movement for Human Rights and the Southern Christian Leadership Council (SCLC) launched the Birmingham Campaign. Dr. King and Fred Shuttlesworth were arrested less than nine days after it began. While in jail, Dr. King prompted by the release of "A Call to Unity"—an open letter that had been published by eight white clergyman—wrote and later published his "Letter from a Birmingham Jail. In the Call, the clergyman argued that King and other outsiders should not involve themselves in what was happening in the city of Birmingham; and, that the struggle for civil rights belonged in the courtrooms and not in the streets.[21]

King's "Letter," which had been written on the scraps of newspaper and smuggled out by Rev. Wyatt T. Walker, answered this call and served as a moral edict on the spiritual consciousness of our nation. I do not understand how you can read that letter and not be moved. He wrote that we are caught in an "inescapable network of mutuality, tied in a single garment of destiny. Whatever affects one directly, affects all indirectly."[22] Who could, after reading this letter, be silent and risk having their silence mistaken for complicity? We read that letter today and forget that it is calling us to do something, to go farther than we ever thought possible, to realize that our stories are connected and intricately tied to the stories that are being told around the world so the suffering in South Carolina is tied to the suffering in Syria; the struggle to free Marissa Alexander and Mumia Abu Jamal is just as important as the struggle to free Aung San Suu Kyi; and, the images of college students being pepper-sprayed at UC Davis are just as significant and important as the images of the women being sprayed with tear gas in Taksim Square in Turkey. Injustice anywhere—whether in Florida, North Carolina, Turkey, Sudan, or Sandy Hook—is a threat to justice everywhere, a statement that is as true today as it was when Dr. King first wrote them. He talked about the policy of nonviolent resistance that had been practiced by Jesus Christ, Mahatma Gandhi, and James Farmer; and when the letter was released, a gear shifted.

Less than a month later, the children begin to speak: high school, middle, and elementary school children trained in nonviolent resistance, inspired by the Movement, and believing in the push for justice became actively involved in the Birmingham Campaign. They were arrested so often that going to prison was probably something that became a part of their daily agenda and they were committed to it: "So, you wake up in the morning, you wash your face, you go to prison. You get back out. You wake up in the morning, go to school, go to prison, get back out." It was part of what they were doing, and they were committed to it.

These children were actively involved. They were foot soldiers who have been called the Movement's secret weapon. Who would have expected that the leaders of the Movement would have allowed children to be on the front line? The images that documented the attacks were devastating. They were shocking, and they moved and impacted the world.

Although some people believe that only the consciousness of America was shifted after the pictures were released, I believe that the consciousness of the entire world was shifted. When people saw what happened to those children and watched the interviews where witnesses stated that Bull Conner complained that the police dogs were not vicious enough, it is easy to understand how gears began to shift. In an interview with the National Visionary Leadership Project (NVLP), Dick Gregory said that when he arrived in Birmingham, he was arrested before he had a chance to do anything. He said that this was not unusual because whenever the local police heard that he was coming to a city, they would send the paddy wagon to the airport to pick him up. When he was arrested in Birmingham, he shared a cell with a four-year-old boy. Gregory said he asked him, "Why are you here? What do you want?" The little boy said, "Teetum. I just want my teetum."[23] Gregory was surprised because even though the little boy could not pronounce the word "freedom," he knew what he wanted. If a four-year-old boy can stand up for what is right and be an active participant in the movement for freedom and justice and equality, why can't you? You do not have to be old to stand up for the right thing.

These children were freedom fighters. Their active genius—their ability to create and produce—had been sparked and they had been set loose upon the world. The children in Birmingham believed that freedom (similar to what our ancestors who left the plantations in 1863 believed) was something that you had to go and get. Run if you have to, crawl if you must, but freedom, justice, and equality are out there and we have to get there. If you keep moving, eventually the bending moral arc will reach its mark.

We also celebrated the fiftieth anniversary of the March on Washington for Jobs and Freedom where over 250,000 people—black and white; men, women, and children—met in Washington, DC, in front of the Lincoln Memorial, in response to a Call that had been set forth by the leaders of the major African-American organizations. They were called the Big Six and the group consisted of James Farmer from the Congress of Racial Equality (CORE); King, who led the Southern Christian Leadership Conference (SCLC); John Lewis from the Student Nonviolent Coordinating Committee (SNCC); A. Philip Randolph from the Brotherhood of Sleeping Car Porters; Roy Wilkins from the National Association for the Advancement of Colored People (NAACP); and Whitney Young, Jr., from the National Urban League. It is important to note that this title (the "Big Six") is actually inaccurate because Dorothy I. Height, the president of the National Council of Negro Women, was present at almost every meeting. She was at the table, and though she was not allowed to speak at the March and history often fails to include her contributions to the planning of the event, we must be the ones who remember her. They should have been called the "Big Seven," and those of us who know the history, who love the history, and who refuse to be erased from the history must always include everybody who was at the table, and that includes her. So the "Big Seven" told the people to come and they did. They walked, they ran; they came in cars, on buses, on trailers, whatever it took to get there because they believed that something was going to happen in Washington, DC. They believed that lives were going to be changed, gears were going to be shifted, and genius was going to be sparked.

I remember when my father told me about the March on Washington. He was in the military in DC, and he heard that the military was planning to close the base on Saturday morning so that nobody could leave to attend the March. My father and his friend decided to leave on Friday night because, "They're not going to keep me from being a part of history. I am not going to look back one day and say I wish I was there, but I wasn't." He was there, and he said his life was fundamentally changed.

"Being there," he said, "was like getting a shot in your arm and feeling the medicine work its way up your arm into your chest." He said that it got to his chest and began to move down the other arm. He felt it move from his arm into his stomach and that by the time it got to his feet, all he could think about was change:

> I knew that I needed to do something different because change was coming and I've got to do something. I've got to be better. I've got to go farther. I've got to get my kids ready because change is coming, and even if I can't be there, there's got to be a Wise at the table. There must be someone from the Wise family sitting at the table. And even if it takes one hundred years, it is ok because my kids will know how to prepare their kids and this family will continue. We will go forward and we will be ready when freedom comes.

My father was right: we *must* be ready when freedom comes. When it comes, we will enjoy it because we have been working for it all our lives. It is a part of our blood; it is part of our system; it is part of the soil; it is part of the earth; and, it is part of who we are. We have been working for freedom all our lives, and when it gets here, we need to be ready. This bending moral arc of justice? We have been pushing it towards the end, and we have to be ready when the end comes.

We also commemorated two other events—two very significant moments when our hearts just stopped; two overwhelming moments when we felt like we were like Sisyphus at the bottom of a mountain trying to roll a boulder of justice and equality up a narrow mountain of racism, injustice and unchecked violence; two events when the ground moved underneath us, and we had to remind ourselves that when all else is sinking sand, we have got to stand on solid ground. The first happened when Medgar Evers was assassinated outside of his home in Jackson, Mississippi and the second was when the four little girls—Addie Mae Collins, Cynthia Wesley, Carole Robertson, and Denise McNair—were killed inside the Sixteenth Street Baptist Church. (I remember a time when churches and front yards used to be safe grounds.)[24] When these two events happened, it felt as if things were sinking and shifting underneath the Movement, and it took everything they had to remain solid, but they did. They stayed anchored. They stayed rooted. They stood on the solid rock. They knew that they were going to lose some folks along the way, unfortunately; but that when freedom comes, there must be somebody at the end to greet it. And that is where we come in: we must be ready.

I believe that the first step to sparking genius is learning how to recognize the truth. There are many versions of the truth and once you accept one, you must taste it, hold it up to the light, and ruthlessly examine it for yourself. You must challenge the truth, scrutinize it, test it and then, when you are sure that what you believe to be the truth actually is, you must move forward and share it with others. You must also be willing to forgive yourself if you later find out that your understanding of the truth has in fact been rendered false.

Next, you must learn how to see and dream beyond your current situation. I once asked my father how do you learn how to do this and more importantly, how do you teach others how to do it. He told me a story about a man who wanted his servants to build him a boat. Since the workers had never seen a boat or the ocean, the man was having a difficult time getting them motivated to start the work. When he told his wife about his dilemma, she told him to stop talking to his crew about building the boat and instead take them down to the ocean just as the sun begins to set. Once they get there, have them take off their shoes so that they can feel the water beneath their feet. Tell them to put their hands in the sand so they can see how it feels to have it run through their fingers. Tell them to close their eyes and concentrate on smelling the salt water. And then, when the moon begins to look as if it is rising out of the water, have them open their eyes and think about what it must be like to go out on the water, beyond where their eyes can see. If you do that, she told him, then you do not ever have to talk about building a boat again because they will run back, get the equipment, and start working as quickly as they can. When someone has seen as far as their eye can see, then they are going to want to see beyond.

There is a place that exists beyond our current reality, beyond our unfulfilled dreams and broken promises, beyond poverty and crime and illiteracy and abuse, a place that exists— only at this moment—in our dreams. A place that we can only get to by sparking genius, shifting gears, and changing the current narrative. We must work together to spark the genius in our young people at the same time that we are (re)sparking the genius in ourselves. I know that some of us have been running for quite a long time, and we have gotten a little weary; we have walked at times and we may be a little bit faint. But our journey has not ended and our jobs are still needed. As long as you are here, you are needed and the work must be done and must be done by you.

ASALH family, I challenge you today to see beyond what your eye can see—to see to that place in time where the moral arc has stopped bending and justice and equality are the norm.

I challenge you today in the spirit of Carter G. Woodson and Martin Luther King, Jr., Langston Hughes and James Baldwin, Dorothy I. Height and Mary McLeod Bethune to join with me and to lean into that space; and as we collectively press forward for the mark of the high calling that we push forward with one hand and we reach back and grab somebody else's hand with the other.

We will get there, ASALH, but we must be committed to getting there together. Thank you!

# *Conra Gist*

*"Teachers must be challenged to see beyond what their eyes can see"*

The Woodson Lecture sounds like a battle cry alerting the audience of danger. A concerned and passionate voice seeks to galvanize the intellectual base towards faith in the long arm of justice. Proclamations of the arduous work necessary for any group committed to realizing social justice is vividly illustrated. Seeing the moral arc return to justice, however, is not inevitable; the outcome requires a certain consciousness that compels action. Through the performative act of conscious raising, a strategy that has proven essential to any social justice effort, Whitehead shares personal small-moment narratives to illustrate lessons about justice. The narratives speak of past exhortations of a father who raises a daughter to be a difference maker in the world. They tell of a present in which the intricate web of humanity is infected with a network of global inequality. They offer a window through which to see a mother aspiring to raise sons who will be men poised to see beyond what the eye can see. No matter the perspective in time, each narrative pursues a possible path to justice.

The battle cry is characterized by a spiritual epistemology that frames humanity as potential reconcilers for what is right in an immoral world. Collins explains, "The moral authority that emerges from this type of spirituality becomes increasingly significant in a secular world grounded in the commodity relations associated with profound injustices."[25] Implicit is a deep conviction in the divine hand of justice who involves humanity in a type of spiritual struggle for establishing the right order of things in the world. Justice is the place where "the crooked," according to Whitehead, quoting Dr. King, "has been made straight."[26] Justice motivates people to "be like David who ran to meet Goliath confident." When people cannot run, and there is "sinking sand all around," justice requires that people "stand on the solid rock." Submitting to justice, humans commit to service, acting as "living sacrifices" that stay on course by "pressing forward for the mark of the high calling."[27] The Woodson Lecture awakens a deep spiritual connectivity through a moral imperative. Simultaneously, the battle cry also articulates a clear set of conscience-raising behaviors—shifting narratives, sparking genius, and learning how to see beyond— that concretize humanity's obligatory relationship with justice. Readers are challenged to respond by embracing the work of justice in their professional and personal lives. The citing of alarming statistics on student achievement, the school-to-prison pipeline, and youth violence, however, are particularly salient for educators.

Teachers are key levers in the education enterprise, and education plays a critical role in any social justice effort. For example, the act of conscience raising taps the psycho-social-emotional domains of intellect to inspire a change in thinking. In the classroom, learning involves interacting with socially mediated and constructed knowledge, skills, and/ or understandings that, when meaningfully and responsively embedded in students' lives, can elicit a positive change in their capacity to engage and potentially transform the society in which they live. Teachers who decide to oblige the call of justice will have to commit to redefine their position, power, and privilege in schools. Collins describes, "The turning point or threshold at which hype turns into reality constitutes the onset of a critical mass."[28] If teachers are positioned as a critical mass in education, this prompts the question, how does this spiritual epistemology of justice inform the work of teachers in schools? In an effort to connect the justice seekers in the battle cry to the cultural work of teaching and learning in schools, the following section explores three identity markers that characterize educators who teach for social justice.

## *Teachers as visionaries*

Whitehead's assertion that justice seekers must "see beyond" is a curious challenge. Our educational system is becoming increasingly outcomes based, focused primarily on identifying and eliminating problems to develop more efficient and profitable schools. One unfortunate consequence of this shift in focus is that the public discourse on teaching and learning situates teachers as problems to be solved. Teachers are under increasing surveillance and discipline through contentious reform efforts such as teacher value-added performance measures. In an attempt to walk the tightrope of accountability, teachers can foster unhealthy teacher identities rooted in equations that attempt to determine their value utilizing limited and narrow data sets. Yet, it is here a justice seeker's charge to learn how to see beyond is instructive. Teachers must see beyond the scrutiny of accountability and "search for goodness" in their students, schools, and local communities.[29] Visionaries see what others cannot see or refuse to see. Even if the current educational system does not "see" teachers as visionaries and does not reward them for their vision, teachers still must see themselves as such.

As encouragement Whitehead offers this charge: "...I challenge you today to see beyond what your eye can see—to see to that place and time where the moral arc has stopped bending and justice and equality are the norm." For teachers this means seeing the day when the erasure of the achievement gap is realized, the provision of equitable funding across schools and resources is enforced, and critically engaged and informed citizenry in local school communities work collectively to improve the quality of their lives. If teachers are to lead students, they must have a vision of a world in which justice reigns. Perhaps in this sense, grading papers, recommending students for advanced placement, calling parents, late-night curriculum planning, early-morning tutorials, and Saturday professional development sessions can all be viewed as opportunities to enact justice by working towards what is right. Then, these responsibilities do not comprise a list of duties in the job description of a teacher; instead, they can quite possibly be individual subversive acts of justice that may make children's lives better or increase their chances of realizing dreams they are scared to dream. Teachers are no longer problems to be solved but visionaries who model the work of justice. Imagine a society in which teachers are a critical mass of mathematicians, scientists, writers, historians, and theorists who fight for justice in the classroom each day. In the face of stories of inadequacy that dominate schooling discourse, the justice worker may be required not only to see beyond but also to believe justice is an attainable goal.

## *Teachers as trailblazers*

If teachers are visionaries, then it will not be enough for them to reimagine daily tasks of teaching as justice acts; nor will it be sufficient to dream of a world of equality. It will also require actively paving a trail for justice. In his "Letter from a Birmingham Jail," King is troubled by the stagnation and silence of the justice workers for the right, noting the following:

> More and more I feel that the people of ill will have used time much more effectively than have the people of good will. We will have to repent in this generation not merely for the hateful words and actions of the bad people but for the appalling silence of the good people. Human progress never rolls in on wheels of inevitability; it comes through the tireless efforts of men willing to be co-workers with God, and without this hard work, time itself becomes an ally of the forces of social stagnation. We must use time creatively, in the knowledge that the time is always ripe to do right.[30]

Of King's "Letter," Whitehead asks, "Who could, after reading it, be silent and risk having their silence mistaken for complicity?" The leaders of the accountability movement have clearly framed a sense of urgency to make swift and sweeping changes. Statistics on the failure of a defunct evaluation system are being utilized to transform the professionalization of teachers. Though it is easy to take issue with the approach, the urgency expressed by reformers is coupled with action that is clear and resolute. This begs the question, what are the urgent concerns of teachers for social justice? How can teachers shift the dominant narrative of teachers as compliers to a narrative of teachers as trailblazers for social justice? According to Whitehead, regarding making a shift in narrative, "…the moments in history that define who we are, these are the moments that shift our cultural narrative, disrupt what is considered to be the norm, and that collectively move us onto a different path."

Teachers' passivity and acceptance of injustice must be disrupted with action. Gist, Flores, and Claeys developed a Critical Teacher Development Theory (CTDT) based on the work of teachers of color who resist symbolic acts of violence that attempt to undermine the usefulness of their cultural and linguistic knowledge systems in pedagogy and professional development.[31] Specifically, the CTDT theorizes teacher learning as an iterative socio-constructivist process in which teachers work as change agents in knowledge-centered communities of practice who assess, implement, and refine rigorous and culturally responsive pedagogy for the students most often marginalized in schools. Thus, as a critical mass, teachers are trailblazers who walk the road to justice by (1) acting as change agents for what is right in schools, (2) participating in diverse professional knowledge-centered communities of practice, and (3) consistently working to strengthen pedagogical approaches that increase educational attainment for students often denied the dignity and hope of a culturally and linguistically responsive education. Narratives of teacher pathology can shift to narratives of teachers as justice workers when teachers are viewed as those who regularly engage in intellectual work, have a healthy love for learning, and teach and learn in active professional communities.

## *Teachers as genius sparkers*

It is reasonable to conclude that a shift in the framing of teacher identity from problem to trailblazer also assumes a shift in the expectations of students. No one would argue that student achievement is not important. Yet, when student achievement is limited to a single variable for defining student success, we unwittingly limit students' (and society's) understanding of the learning process and the practice of excellence. Whitehead describes genius as, "inspiration" or "talent," which means you are not born a genius; it is something that you become, that you work at. "It is a goal. It is attainable, and it is something that sits right out there in front of you." When genius is sparked, then, it is marked by a change in how students see themselves interfacing with and eventually changing the world around them.

The language in two current influential reform efforts, Common Core State Standards (CCSS) and the Framework for Effective (FfT) teaching, rely heavily on a teacher's ability to spark genius in students. For example, the CCSS offers portrait statements of students for ELA & literacy in history/ social studies, science, and technical subjects, three of which portray the importance of a students' ability to 1) respond to the varying demands of audience, task, purpose, and discipline; 2) demonstrate independence; and 3) build strong content knowledge. In each of these actions, students are placed at the center as the primary creator, facilitator, and actor in the learning process. Students must make meaning of content through a process that allows them to internalize and produce representations of their understandings. The teacher, however, must spark genius and motivation to encourage this process to take place. Similarly, in the case of the FfT, the instructional domains rate educators' ability to establish transference of learning from the teacher to the student as distinguished practice. According to FfT, distinguished practice comes at the point in which students are, for instance, asking questions, assessing and engaging in reflections about content and learning, and actively working to establish a culture for learning in the classroom. As is the case in both the content (CCSS) and the instructional domains (FfT), each framework depends on the teachers' ability to spark students' genius if the goals of either are to be realized.

Teaching for social justice equips teachers with the charge to model growth mindsets about student learning.[32] A teacher who sparks genius sees ability as a starting point, focuses on developing student passion, uncovers mistakes and challenges students to learn from them, and views effort as a vital ingredient for growth. In this sense, teachers who spark genius halt the practice of shaming in classrooms and replace it with the practice of grit. When students value effort and learn to persist in the face of challenge, they foster a personal resilience that equips them to pursue their genius.

## *A spiritual epistemology of justice*

When the themes of the battle cry are applied, teachers are visionaries who, in pursuit of justice through everyday individual and collective subversive acts, blaze trails in practitioner communities of solidarity to spark genius in students. The spiritual epistemology of justice can in fact be utilized as a lens through which to interpret teachers' cultural work and agency in schools. Specifically, this lens, when combined with the work of teachers, envisions teachers as a critical mass of reconcilers who work to engage schools in a transformative relationship with justice. As justice seekers they commit to struggle and overcome seemingly insurmountable obstructions to just schools. Whitehead's characterization of justice seekers like "David who ran to meet Goliath confident" is similar to teachers who resolve to confront intimidating obstacles. Recognizing the difficult yet vital responsibility of justice seekers, teachers are able to see classrooms and schools as spaces and sites where justice can grow and live or, in other words, see the "place where the crooked has been made straight." To perceive classrooms and schools as battlegrounds for justice requires an empowered mindset of action—a "pressing forward for the mark of the high calling." Teachers draw from a deep reservoir of conviction to motivate them to commit daily justice acts as "living sacrifices" despite the hopelessness that is "the sinking sand all around" them in the form of unjust policies and practices in the educational system. All of this is possible in the spiritual epistemology of justice because teachers (justice seekers) answer the call to work to make the world right. No matter your vocation, Whitehead suggests the path of justice is available to all. Will you answer the call?

# At the Crossroads of Emancipation and Freedom

## *Lesson Plan*

**Intended Audience:** Middle and High School Students

**Overview:** This lesson examines some of the Critical Moments in American history that happened in 1863 and in 1963 that define and expand our understanding of emancipation and freedom. Using Whitehead's Woodson Lecture as a lens, students will evaluate and explore five Critical Moments, including the release of the Emancipation Proclamation; the March on Washington; the Birmingham Campaign (Project C) and the subsequent release of Dr. Martin Luther King, Jr.'s "Letter from a Birmingham Jail"; and the bombing of the Sixteenth Street Baptist Church in Birmingham, Alabama.

**Scope and Sequence:** The order and structure of this lesson may be adjusted, so educators should make adjustments as needed to adapt the lesson to their classroom. Students will read the Woodson Lecture and examine videos, photos, and audio sources to help place the events into a larger context. Each of the Critical Moments can be expanded into complete lessons or used as warm-ups during a one-week daily teach-in on emancipation and freedom. Students that have access to the internet should be encouraged to conduct independent research on the Critical Moments to enhance their understanding of the moments and the importance of the early and the modern Civil Rights Movement.

## *National Standards for History*[33]
Standard 3: Historical Analysis and Interpretation

B. Consider multiple perspectives of various peoples in the past by demonstrating their differing motives, beliefs, interests, hopes and fears.

H. Hold interpretations of history as tentative, subject to changes as new information is added.

### Common Core State Standards[34]

- CCSS.ELA-Literacy.RH.6-8.1 Cite specific textual evidence to support analysis of primary and secondary sources.
- CCSS.ELA-Literacy.RH.6-8.2 Determine the central ideas or information of a primary or secondary source; provide an accurate summary of the source distinct from prior knowledge or opinions.

## *Objectives*
At the end of lesson, students will be able to do the following:

1. Discuss some of the Critical Moments that happened during the early and the modern Civil Rights Movement, focusing particularly on 1863 and 1963.
2. Debate and identify the strengths and weaknesses of these Critical Moments through comparative analysis.
3. Evaluate the merits of these Critical Moments while placing them in a broader historical context.
4. Determine and explain how these Critical Moments set the stage for how we currently define and understand emancipation and freedom.

## Introduction

The 2013 Black History Month theme, suggested by the Association for the Study of African-American Life and History (ASALH) and adopted by the White House, was "At the Crossroads of Emancipation and Freedom." It was designed to connect the release of the Emancipation Proclamation on January 1, 1863, to the March on Washington for Jobs and Freedom that happened one hundred years later on August 28, 1963. The marchers met at the Lincoln Memorial and more than one speaker, including Dr. King, connected Abraham Lincoln and the release of the Proclamation to the March. Although both events were historic, the March took place during a year when several Critical Moments occurred that shaped the direction of the modern Civil Rights Movement. In April, at the beginning of the Birmingham Campaign (Project C) after Dr. King was arrested, eight clergymen in the city released "A Call for Unity," arguing that outsiders should not involve themselves in the state's issues and that the fight for civil rights should happen in the courtrooms and not on the streets. In response, King—with help from Rev. Wyatt T. Walker—wrote and released his "Letter from a Birmingham Jail," which explained his involvement in the Birmingham struggle and which quickly became a moral compass for both the United States and the world. Additionally, the Birmingham Campaign marked the first time when organizers decided to train elementary, middle, and high school students to become involved in and march on the front lines. This organized student protest, the Children's Crusade, resulted in hundreds of students being brutally attacked, arrested, and sprayed with water hoses; and, the photographs documenting these atrocities were seen around the world. [35] The outrage to these incidents led to President John F.

Kennedy's involvement and set the stage for his June 11th Civil Rights Address and his drafting of the Civil Rights Act, which was passed in 1964. One day later, Medgar Evers, the head of the NAACP branch in Jackson, Mississippi, was assassinated outside of his home. The March took place in August and on September 15th, at the Sixteenth Century Baptist where the meetings had been held during Project C, members of the Ku Klux Klan bombed the church killing four little girls—Addie Mae Collins, Cynthia Wesley, Carole Robertson, and Denise McNair.

One hundred years after the release of the Emancipation Proclamation, African Americans were still fighting every single day to overcome the systemic nature of racism, injustice, inequality, and discrimination. A close examination of these Critical Moments will aid students in connecting them together and placing them in a broader historical context. This lesson plan effectively uses Whitehead's Woodson Lecture as a lens through which students can enter into this important conversation. Additionally, this lesson plan seeks to place the students, in the words of Gist, "at the center as the primary creator, facilitator, and actor in the learning process" to help them closely examine and reevaluate the impact of these Critical Moments from their unique perspectives. Through this type of comparative study, students will become active agents of their own learning by offering solutions, challenging misconceptions, and advancing this important ongoing discussion about emancipation and freedom.

# *Documents* [36]

## *The Emancipation Proclamation*
- Document: http://www.archives.gov/exhibits/featured_documents/emancipation_proclamation/ 37
- Excerpt from John Hope Franklin's "The Emancipation Proclamation: An Act of Justice": http://www.archives.gov/publications/prologue/1993/summer/emancipation-proclamation.html 38

## *The Birmingham Campaign*
- President Kennedy's response to the Birmingham Campaign: http://www.pbs.org/wgbh/amex/eyesontheprize/ sources/ps_c.html 39
- The Birmingham Campaign: http://mlk-kpp01.stanford.edu/index.php/encyclopedia/encyclopedia/enc_birmingham_campaign/40

## *Letter from a Birmingham Jail*
- Dr. King's Letter: http://mlk-kpp01.stanford.edu/index.php/encyclopedia/documentsentry/annotated_letter_from_birmingham/41
- "MLK's Letter from a Birmingham Jail – 'A Call for Unity; (1963)" http://www.youtube.com/

watch?v=S83jYXYTwHw and http://www.stanford.edu/ group/King//frequentdocs/clergy.pdf 42
- Frequently Requested Documents. The Estate of Martin Luther King, Jr. "Statement by Alabama Clergymen." 43
- Wyatt T. Walker, "Project C." http://www.youtube.com/ watch?v=dL2RZ2Ic4dY

## *The March on Washington*
- "The March on Washington: Power to the People." http:// life.time.com/history/march-on-washington-photos-from-an-epic-civil-rights-event/#145
- Transcript, "Dr. Martin Luther King, Jr. 'I Have a Dream' Speech." http://www.foxnews.com/us/2013/08/27/ transcript-martin-luther-king-jr-have-dream-speech/46
- "Martin Luther King – I Have a Dream, August 28, 1963" http://www.youtube.com/watch?v=HRIF4_WzU1w47
- "Rep. John Lewis Recalls His Speech at the March on Washington." http://www.youtube.com/watch?v=MFUI-at4sEg48

## *The Bombing at 16th Street Baptist Church*
- "Birmingham, Alabama, and the Civil Rights Movement in 1963" http://www.english.illinois.edu/maps/poets/m_r/ randall/birmingham.htm49

## *Discussion Points*
1. How did the release of the Emancipation Proclamation lead to the ending of the Civil War and the ratification of the Thirteenth Amendment? Identify and discuss two events that happened in the enslaved and free black community immediately after the Proclamation was released.

2. How did the Critical Moments that happened in 1963 shape the direction of the modern Civil Rights Movement?

3. Explain how the events that happened during the Birmingham Campaign led to the release of "A Call for Unity." How did Dr. King's arrest and the release of the "Call" lead to his writing and publishing his "Letter from a Birmingham Jail"? How did Dr. King's arrest at the beginning of the Campaign influence the decision to allow children to be on the front line of the Movement?

4. Outline the purpose of the March on Washington explaining why it was so important for everyone to come and participate in it. Why is Dorothy I. Height usually not included as one of the leaders who shaped and planned the March? Compare John Lewis written speech to his spoken word, and explain why you think they encouraged him to change it.

5. How did the Birmingham Campaign, "A Call for Unity," and the "Letter" lead to the events that happened at the 16th Street Baptist Church? What are some of the lessons that can be learned from the bombing of the church?

## *At the Crossroads*

### Motivation

1. Tell the students that they going to spend the next two days talking about emancipation and freedom by examining the 1863 release of the Emancipation Proclamation, during the early Civil Rights Movement, and some of the Critical Moments that happened in 1963, during the modern Civil Rights Movement.

2.  Activate prior knowledge by asking the students to share what they know about the early and the modern Civil Rights Movement.

3.  Have students watch a clip from the "Fighting Back 1957-1962" episode from the *Eyes on the Prize* documentary which outlines events that happened in the Civil Rights Movement prior to 1963.

4.  After they watch the clip, have students write a short reflection on the Civil Rights Movement, sharing some of the ways they think that the Movement changed our country.

5.  Using the Woodson Lecture and the Introduction in the lesson plan, take a few minutes to present a Lecture Blast that discusses the Emancipation Proclamation and highlights the Critical Moments that happened in 1963.

    *Take a moment to clear up misconceptions that students may have about either The Emancipation Proclamation or the Critical Moments.*

6.  Once finished, have students review their reflection and share them with the class.

## Shared Activity

7.  Have students work in groups of two or three to go through each one of the Critical Moments and define and explain how it happened and what were the pros and cons of the event. Depending upon how much time is allocated for the independent research, student groups can work through all of the Critical Moments or select a few.

8.  Student groups should prepare a PowerPoint

presentation to share out their findings.

## Wrap-up

9. To close the discussion, students should revisit the Discussion Points to discuss and debate during a whole-group discussion.

# *Biographies*

**Calvin Coleman** is a self-taught artist who incorporates abstract expressionism and Fauvism; Coleman builds upon the canvas with an assemblage of heavy body acrylic paint, a variety of textiles and other mediums to embellish his uninhibited style of painting. After graduating from Lincoln University, where he earned his B.S. degree in Early Childhood Education, Coleman taught at the elementary level for fourteen years. Works by Calvin Coleman are included in numerous public, private collections and publications including the Embassy of Rome, Italy, and the permanent collection of the City of Atlanta Housing and Urban Development; Lincoln University (PA); and Drexel University.

**Conra D. Gist, Ph.D.**, is an assistant professor of Curriculum and Instruction at the University of Arkansas. She received her Ph.D. from the City University of New York (CUNY). Her primary research interests focus on teacher diversity, culturally responsive pedagogy, and teacher learning.

**Ronald D. Harrison, Jr., M.Div.**, is the MI-BEST program coordinator at Baltimore City Community College, Baltimore, Maryland. His more than fifteen years in education include work as senior administrator and vice-principal of two private schools in Baltimore and Upper Marlboro. His interests include teacher development, theology, and ancient languages. He provided editorial support for Whitehead's book, *Notes from a Colored Girl: The Civil War Pocket Diaries of Emilie Frances Davis* (USC Press, 2014).

**Alicia L. Moore, Ph.D.,** holds the Cargill Endowed Professorship in Education at Southwestern University, Georgetown, Texas. She is the Co-Editor for the Association for the Study of African American Life and History's <u>Black History Bulletin</u> (BHB).

**La Vonne I. Neal, Ph.D.,** is dean of the College of Education and a professor of special education at Northern Illinois University. She is the Co-Editor for the Association for the Study of African American Life and History's <u>Black History Bulletin</u> (BHB).

**Karsonya (Kaye) Wise Whitehead, Ph.D.,** is an assistant professor of Communication and African and African-American Studies at Loyola University Maryland. She is a former award-winning middle school teacher, the 2006-07 Gilder Lehrman Maryland History Teacher of the Year, and a three-time New York Emmy-nominated documentary filmmaker. She is the author of two forthcoming books, *Notes from a Colored Girl: The Civil War Pocket Diaries of Emilie Frances Davis* (USC Press, 2014) and *The Emancipation Proclamation: Race Relations on the Eve of Reconstruction* (Routledge, 2014).

# *Bibliography*

### Books by and about Carter G. Woodson

Donaldson, Bobby J. *"Circles of Learning": Exploring the Library of Carter G. Woodson.* The Journal of African American History, Vol. 93, No. 1 (Winter, 2008). Association for the Study of African American Life and History, Inc.: 80-87.

Greene, Lorenzo J. and Carter Godwin Woodson. *The Negro wage earner.* New York: Russell & Russell, 1969.

Logan, Rayford W. *Carter G. Woodson: Mirror and Molder of His Time, 1875-1950.* The Journal of Negro History, Vol. 58, No. 1 (Jan., 1973). Association for the Study of African American Life and History, Inc.: 1-17.

Wesley, Charles Harris. *Recollections of Carter G. Woodson.* The Journal of Negro History, Vol. 83, No. 2 (Spring, 1998). Association for the Study of African American Life and History, Inc.: 143-148,

Winston, Michael R. *Carter Godwin Woodson: Prophet of a Black Tradition.* The Journal of Negro History, Vol. 60, No. 4 (Oct., 1975). Association for the Study of African American Life and

History, Inc.: 459-463.

Woodson, Carter Godwin. *The African background outlined; or, Handbook for the study of the Negro.* New York: Negro Universities Press, [c1936], 1968.

———. *A century of Negro migration.* New York: Russell & Russell, 1969.

———. *The Education of the Negro Prior to 1861; A History of the Education of the Colored People of the United States from the Beginning of Slavery to the Civil War.* Washington, DC: Associated Publishers, c1919.

———. *Free Negro Owners of Slaves in the United States in 1830, together with Absentee ownership of slaves in the United States in 1830.* New York: Negro Universities Press, [c1924], 1968

———. *The Mind of the Negro as Reflected in Letters Written During the Crisis, 1800-1860.* New York: Negro Universities Press, 1969.

———. *The Mis-education of the Negro.* New York: AMS Press, 1977.

———. *The Rural Negro.* New York: Russell & Russell, 1969.

———. *The Story of the Negro Retold.* Washington, DC: The Associated Publishers, Inc., 1935.

Woodson, Carter G. and Charles H Wesley. *Negro Makers of History.* Washington, DC: Associated Publishers, Inc., c1968.

———. *The Negro in Our History*. Washington, DC: Associated Publishers, 1972.

# *Endnotes*

1. References to Whitehead's 2013 Carter G. Woodson Lecture are from her spoken lecture given at the Association for the Study of African American Life and History (ASALH) on October 9, 2013. An audiotaped version of the speech and the transcript are both available at www.kayewisewhitehead. com.

2. First Parrish in Concord, "Theodore Parker Puts Freedom of Conscience to the Test."

3. Baldwin, James. "A Letter to My Nephew." The Progressive, December 1962 Issue. http://progressive.org/archive/1962/december/letter (accessed 8 December 2013)

4. Dr. Martin Luther King, Jr. "Speech in Montgomery, Alabama, 1965." http://www.youtube.com/watch?v=IIT0ra9-mTc (accessed 4 November 2013)

5. "Letter from a Birmingham Jail." The Martin Luther King, Jr. Research and Education Institute. http://mlk-kpp01. stanford.edu/index.php/resources/article/annotated_letter_from_birmingham/ (accessed 8 December 2013)

6. Woodson, Carter G. *The Mis-Education of the Negro*. Edited with an Introduction by Charles H. Wesley and Thelma D. Perry. First Published in 1933.

7. This speech was delivered on October 7, 2013, and changes

were made during the delivery. www.kayewisewhitehead. com.

8. First Parrish in Concord.

9. King, Jr. "Speech in Montgomery, Alabama, 1965."

10. Historic Documents, "Martin Luther King, Jr.'s I Have a Dream Speech." March on Washington, DC, August 28, 1963.

11. King, Martin Luther, Jr. "Non-Violence and Racial Justice." In *Christian Century*, February 6, 1957.

12. On July 13, in the *State of Florida v. George Zimmerman* trial, a jury of six women voted to acquit George Zimmerman of second-degree murder and manslaughter charges in the death of Trayvon Martin. In the *Shelby County, Alabama v. Holder, Attorney General, et al* ruling, the United States Supreme Court stuck down a key portion of the 1965 Voting Rights Act, essentially freeing nine states, mostly in the South, to change their election laws without advance federal approval. http://www.supremecourt.gov/opinions/12pdf/12-96_6k47.pdf (accessed 11 November 2013)

13. "Yes We Can. The Schott 50 State Report on Publication Education and Black Males 2010." Schott Foundation for Public Education. http://www.blackboysreport.org/bbreport.pdf (accessed 8 December 2013)

14. "4th Graders Who Scored Below Proficient Reading Level by Race." Kids Count Data Center. A project of the Annie E. Casey Foundation. http://datacenter.kidscount.org/data/tables/5126-4th-graders-who-scored-below-proficient-reading-level-by-race?loc=1&loct=2#ranking/1/any/true/867/9/11557 (accessed 8 December 2013)

15. In his book, Woodson writes, "The same educational process

which inspires and stimulates the oppressor with the thought that he is everything and has accomplished everything worthwhile, depresses and crushes at the same time the spark of genius in the Negro by making him feel that his race does not amount to much and never will measure up to the standards of other peoples. The Negro thus educated is a hopeless liability of the race." *The Mis-Education of the Negro*. Edited with an Introduction by Charles H. Wesley and Thelma D. Perry. First Published in 1933.

16. Although this quote has been attributed to Eldridge Cleaver, I have been unable to find the original statement. For example, during the 2005 PBS report from the memorial service for Rosa Parks, Julian Bond said, "Ms. Parks was much, much more than the bus woman. She was much, much more than that. Eldridge Cleaver famously remarked that when she sat down that December day in Montgomery fifty years ago, somewhere in the universe a gear in the machinery had shifted. Rosa Parks shifted the gears of the universe all her life, now she belongs to the universe." In Robert Illes's article, "Rosa Parks at 100: 'The Only Tired I Was, Was Tired of Giving In,'" he writes, "Eldridge Cleaver put it, 'Somewhere in the universe a gear in the machinery had shifted' because of what Rosa Parks did." http://brainrow.com/2005/10/31/she-led-us-in-the-paths-of-righteousness.html http://www.laprogressive.com/rosa-parks-at-100/ (accessed 8 December 2013.

17. Nine months before Rosa Parks famously refused to give up her seat, Claudette Colvin, a 15-year old 11th grader, was arrested in Montgomery for refusing to give up her seat. The NAACP decided not to rally around Colvin and waited for someone else to become the face (and spiritual

consciousness) of the Montgomery Bus Boycott. For more on Colvin and other women before Rosa Parks, see Paul Hendrickson's "The Ladies Before Rosa: Let Us Now Praise Unfamous Women." In Rhetoric & Public Affairs, Vol. 8, No. 2 (Summer 2005): 287-298.

18. Douglass, Frederick. *Life and Times of Frederick Douglass*, as published in 1882. (Scituate, MA: Digital Scanning, Inc., 2001): 429.

19. Transcript of Martin Luther King, Jr.'s "I Have a Dream" speech. Foxnews.com published August 27, 2013. http://www.foxnews.com/us/2013/08/27/transcript-martin-luther-king-jr-have-dream-speech/ (accessed 8 December 2013)

20. Sterling, Dorothy. *We Are Still Your Sisters: Black Women in the Nineteenth Century* (New York: W.W. Norton & Company, 1997), 243.

21. Gist, Conra and Karsonya Wise Whitehead. "Deconstructing Dr. Martin Luther King's 'Letter from a Birmingham Jail' and the Strategy of Nonviolent Resistance." In Black History Bulletin, Vol. 76, No.2, (2013): 6-7.

22. "Letter from a Birmingham Jail."

23. The Dick Gregory Interview, April 29, 2013." Washington, DC: *The National Visionary Leadership Project*, 105-106.

24. Medgar Evers was assassinated on June 12, 1963, and the 16th Street Church was bombed on September 15, 1963.

25. Collins, Patricia Hill. *Fighting words: Black women and the search for justice*. Minneapolis, MN: University of Minnesota, 1988, 244.

26. Historic Documents, "Martin Luther King, Jr.'s I Have a Dream Speech." March on Washington, DC, August 28, 1963.

27. Whitehead, "Sparking the Genius" public lecture.

28. Collins. *Fighting words*, (242).

29. Lawrence-Lightfoot, Sara. "Reflections on portraiture: a dialogue between art and science." Qualitative Inquiry, 11 (1), 2005: 3-15.

30. King, Martin Luther, Jr. "Letter from a Birmingham Jail." In *Liberation: An Independent Monthly*. June, 1963: 10-16, 23; The Martin Luther King, Jr. Research and Education Institute: http://mlk-kpp01.stanford.edu/index.php/resources/article /annotated letter from birmingham/ (accessed 12 December 2013)

31. Gist, Conra D., Belinda Bustos Flores, and Lorena Clayes. "Competing theories of change: culturally responsive communities of practice." In Cristine Sleeter, La Vonne Neal, and Kevin K. Kumashiro (eds.), *Addressing the Demographic Imperative: Recruiting, Preparing, and Retaining a Diverse and Highly Effective Teaching Force*. New York: Routledge, 2014.

32. Dweck, Carol. *Mindset: The Psychology of Success*. New York: Ballentine Books, 2006.

33. All websites were accessed on 12 December 2013; Nation Center for History in the Schools. http://www.nchs.ucla.edu/Standards/

34. Common Core State Standards. http://www.corestandards.org/ELA-Literacy/RH/6-8

35. Additionally, May 8, 1963, has been referred to as "Miracle Sunday," the day the protestors yelled out to the Birmingham firemen that they would stand there allowing water to be sprayed at them until they died. This stance cause a number of firemen to disobey Bull Conner's orders and drop their fire hoses. "'We Stand Here Until We Die:' Freedom Movement Shakes America, Shapes Martin Luther King Jr. http://www.prweb.com/releases/2013/8/

prweb11018314.htm

36. All websites were accessed on 12 December 2013.

37. "The Emancipation Proclamation." National Archives and Records Administration.

38. Franklin, John Hope. "The Emancipation Proclamation: An Act of Justice" in Prologue, Vol. 25, No. 2 (1993).

39. "An Ugly Situation in Birmingham, 1963." Eyes On the Prize: America's Civil Rights Movement 1954-1985.

40. "Birmingham Campaign (1963)." Martin Luther King, Jr. And the Global Freedom Struggle.

41. "Letter from a Birmingham Jail." Martin Luther King, Jr. And the Global Freedom Struggle.

42. Jones, Cory. "The Language of Leadership: Dr. King's Letter from a Birmingham Jail."

43. Newsuem. "Making a Change: Civil Rights and the First Amendment"

44. The National Visionary Leadership Project, "Wyatt T. Walker Interview."

45. "Civil Rights Movement '60." Life, August 28, 1963.

46. Fox News, August 27, 2013.

47. "Martin Luther King – I have a Dream Speech, August 28, 1963"

48. "Rep John Lewis Recalls His Speech at he March on Washington." For more on some of the other leaders from the March on Washington, see "Bayard Rustin." http://www.youtube.com/watch?v=MFUI-at4sEg or "Dorothy Height: My experience in The Civil Rights Movement." http://www.youtube.com/watch?v=W5lJ2VzaOR8

49. "Birmingham, Alabama, and the Civil Rights Movement in 1963." About the 1963 Birmingham Church.

50. "The Civil War: A Film by Ken Burns." http://www.pbs.

org/civilwar/; "Voices from the Days of Slavery." American Memory. http://memory.loc.gov/ammem/collections/voices/

51. "Fighting Back 1957-1962." Eyes on the Prize. Directed by Orlando Bagwell, http://www.youtube.com/watch?v=2a32Uc1oP7s

www.ingramcontent.com/pod-product-compliance
Lightning Source LLC
Chambersburg PA
CBHW070815280326
41934CB00012B/3192